SHORT

WHARFEDALE

YORKSHIRE DALES

PAUL HANNON

waymaster

waymaster guides

Hillside Publications
12 Broadlands
Keighley
West Yorkshire
BD20 6HX

First Published 2003

© Paul Hannon 2003

ISBN 1 870141 74 1

Cover illustration: River Wharfe, Burnsall
Back cover: Kilnsey Crag from near Conistone
(Paul Hannon/Hillslides Picture Library)

Printed by Carnmor Print
95-97 London Road
Preston
Lancashire
PR1 4BA

CONTENTS

INTRODUCTION

Wharfedale is the most popular valley within the Yorkshire Dales National Park, not least of all thanks to its accessibility from the West Yorkshire cities of Leeds and Bradford and their surrounding towns. More importantly, Wharfedale is famed for its natural beauty and character-ful villages, starting points for countless great walks. Most of these walks encounter limestone in some shape or form, be it naturally in craggy outcrops, scars and pavements, or simply forged into the drystone walls that parcel the neat fields surrounding every village. Many of the cottages were built to house lead miners' families, though their flower bedecked gardens present a far less austere scene than their original occupants could envisage.

The Wharfe is formed at Beckermonds by the confluence of Oughtershaw and Greenfield Becks. These opening miles, perhaps the Wharfe's loveliest, are known as Langstrothdale. The upper half of the dale is extremely narrow, the dead flat dale floor between Buckden and Grassington overlooked by steep flanks that quickly rise above walled pastures to rough moorland and fell country. The principal heights overtopping these flanks are Buckden Pike, Great Whernside and Birks Fell, seemingly far removed from the huddled villages at their feet.

The Wharfe's major tributary is the Skirfare, which flows through Littondale to lose its identity near the famous landmark of Kilnsey Crag. Sharing many character-istics of its big brother, its seclusion gives it an intimate, possibly even greater charm. Its principal village of Arncliffe was the original home of TV series *Emmerdale Farm*. While the industry of Wharfedale has always been farming, the 19th century witnessed an extraordinary lead mining boom. Small operations existed all over the dale, though the greatest concentration was on Grassington Moor. Their remains are evident today in spoil heaps, ruined smelt mills and kilns, shafts and levels.

Walkers in Wharfedale are fortunate in that along with Swaledale, they have a great concentration of riverside paths to stroll, and the Dales Way long distance route runs the length of the dale. Though your rambles may be more modest adventures, they will nevertheless take you to a wealth of fascinating locations, with outstanding scenery, history and interest at every turn. Most of these walks can be accessed by bus, the main service from Skipton linking the focal point of Grassington with the higher dale as far as Buckden. Whilst the route description should be sufficient to guide you around each walk, a map is recommended for greater information: Ordnance Survey 1:25,000 scale maps give the finest detail, and Explorers OL2 and OL30 cover all the walks.

USEFUL INFORMATION

•Yorkshire Dales National Park
Colvend, Hebden Road, Grassington, Skipton BD23 5LB
(01756-752748)
•Grassington National Park Centre (01756-752774)
•Skipton Tourist Information (01756-792809)
•Ilkley Tourist Information (01943-602319)
•Yorkshire Dales Society (01943-461938)
(working to protect the area's natural beauty)
•Ramblers' Association
2nd Floor, Camelford House, 87-89 Albert Embankment,
London SE1 7BR (020-7339 8500)
•Traveline - public transport information (0870-6082608)
•National Rail Enquiry Line (08457-484950)

WHARFEDALE
20 Short Scenic Walks

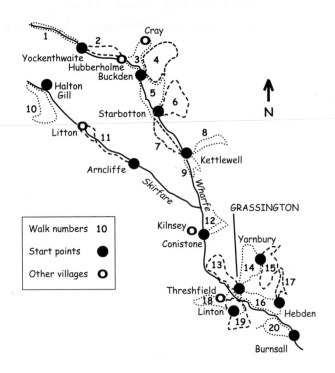

Cray
1
2
Yockenthwaite
Hubberholme
3
4
Buckden
Halton
Gill
5
10
6
Starbotton
Litton
11
8
7
Arncliffe
Skirfare
9
Kettlewell
Wharfe
N

GRASSINGTON

Kilnsey
12
Conistone
Yarnbury

Walk numbers	10
Start points	●
Other villages	○

13
14
15
17
Threshfield
18
16
Linton
19
Hebden
20
Burnsall

A RECORD OF YOUR WALKS

WALK	DATE	NOTES
1	i5	
2	15.4 04	Round trip about 1½ hrs
3	15. 4.04	1½ hrs. to Hubberholme, ¾ hr. back
4		
5		
6		
7		
8		
9		
10		
11		
12		
13		
14		
15		
16		
17		
18		
19		
20		

4³⁄₄ miles   from Yockenthwaite

Peerless walking on the banks of the youthful Wharfe.

• Start: Yockenthwaite Bridge (GR: 904790).
Roadside parking upstream.
• Map: OS Explorer OL30 Yorkshire Dales North/Central.

    Langstrothdale is the name given to the first
miles of the Wharfe, an uncomplicated landscape of farms,
fields and fellsides. The river is no more than a lively
stream, for the most part tinkling rhythmically over a limestone bed. Leave the road by the graceful stone arched
bridge into Yockenthwaite. This farming hamlet enjoys a
magnificent setting, and was named 'Eogan's clearing' by
the Norsemen who settled here. Much later, all this area
was part of the hunting forest of Langstrothdale Chase. Up
to more recent times the small community supported both
an inn and a school.
    Rise up the access track to the first building, but
then turn sharp left to a gate. Here begins a magnificent
ramble in the effervescent company of the infant Wharfe.
Almost at once an old limekiln in good condition is passed.
After a couple of pastures the track fades as it passes
Yockenthwaite stone circle. Easily missed, this compact
grouping of 30 stones is of modest proportion, but in a
noble riverside setting missed by travellers on the road.
From a stile at the field-end beyond it, with a restored
barn ahead, the path rises away from the river through a
wall gap to another stile. Cross the field-top to drop to a
little footbridge at the other side, then on through an old

wall and a little gate to join the access road serving Deepdale, a small farming hamlet.

Turn down to the road and cross the uninspiring bridge, thus neatly keeping the motor road at bay. A track sets forth up the west bank as far as lonely New House, from where a footpath takes over. This is a classic section, a long, unbroken riverbank spell, uninterrupted by gates or stiles, with some nice limestone slabs underfoot. The river, meanwhile, tumbles happily over limestone ledges. By the time a ladder-stile is reached the road has climbed away, so only your footpath keeps faith with the river as far as a wooden footbridge opposite the buildings of Beckermonds.

Beckermonds presides over the meeting of Oughtershaw Beck and Greenfield Beck - the creation of the Wharfe, no less. This confluence below Beckermonds Bridge is reached just yards short of the footbridge. As the walk's turning point, this makes a charming spot for a break on the grassy bank, perhaps being entertained by the antics of wagtails. Beckermonds is backed by the sombre darkness of Greenfield forest, home to a herd of roe deer.

The return options are simple. Either retrace your steps through this lovely landscape, or opt for the narrow road by crossing the bridge, and up a short-lived grassy way to the house. Here turn right on the minor road over the bridge on Oughtershaw Beck and up to the Hawes road at a postbox. The modest mileage to Hawes confirm this isolated settlement's links with that market town, as opposed to its geographical links far down Wharfedale. Turn right along the road, soon dropping down to partner the Wharfe again. For the most part tarmac need not be trodden as the open bank invites steps, to gain a slightly different perspective of the Wharfe from this opposite bank. The same applies after crossing Deepdale Bridge, one can simply shadow the chirpy river on its grassy bank.

3¾ miles   from Yockenthwaite

A classic section of riverbank, and great views too.

•Start: *Yockenthwaite Bridge (GR: 904790).*
Roadside parking upstream.
•Map: *OS Explorer OL30 Yorkshire Dales North/Central.*

Yockenthwaite is a farming hamlet in a magnificent setting: it was named 'Eogan's clearing' by the Norsemen who settled here. Much later, all this area was part of the hunting forest of Langstrothdale Chase. Up to more recent times the small community supported both an inn and a school. Cross the bridge and up the track towards the hamlet, but turn right at the first fork on a track leading above the lowest buildings. Pass through a gate and a couple more just behind, then down to a stile just below. From here a path slants down to join the riverbank. Almost exactly at this point note the lively appearance of a spring, swelling the river from directly under the bank.

The path now shadows the Wharfe downstream in idyllic surrounds, never more than a few steps from its bank. After an enclosed spell, the way opens out into fields again to see Buckden Pike filling the frame ahead. Just beyond a barn the path rises a few feet to negotiate the usually dry Strans Gill by way of a footbridge. Further, as the bank steepens, a path runs along the middle of the scrubby bank, emerging to reveal Hubberholme's church tower literally right in front. The path runs to meet a stony track just behind the church. Turn down it to pass between farm and church to emerge onto the road in Hubberholme.

Barely even a hamlet, Hubberholme claims two famous buildings and a shapely bridge to connect them. The church of St. Michael is a gem: best feature is a 500-year old oak rood loft, one of only two remaining in Yorkshire, while some pews bear the unique trademark of 'Mousy' Thompson. Thus carving, ancient and modern, dominates the highest church in the dale. In an idyllic setting across the river is the whitewashed and timeless *George Inn,* whose snug interior boasts stone flagged floors. This was Bradford author J. B. Priestley's favourite corner, small wonder that he chose to have his ashes scattered here.

The return to Yockenthwaite begins back on the stony track between church and farm, this time remaining on it to climb through pastures to Scar House. Restored in the 19th century, isolated Scar House was the scene of early Quaker gatherings. Pass between the buildings to gain the limestone ledges above. Turn left at the top to a stile by a gate, from where a sketchy path sets an obvious course through the minor outcrops of a limestone shelf.

Passing through a small wood, the path emerges by a footbridge over Strans Gill (again), a limestone ravine with a complex caving system. The path then slants left before resuming a level traverse through numerous walls in various conditions. Some old wall foundations hereabouts suggest this may be the location of an ancient settlement. Throughout this section you enjoy level walking on a super path with outstanding views over Langstrothdale to the Birks Fell-Horse Head ridge, which forms a dark, bulky wall opposite. Yockenthwaite soon appears just below, and then a little further, just beyond an old barn above, it is signed left through the low crumbling wall. It slants down to a wall below before running on through more trees to emerge on a stony track above Yockenthwaite. The track drops down to the hamlet to finish.

4¼ miles   from Buckden

Easy walking through memorable upper dale scenery.

• Start: *Village centre (GR: 942772).*
National Park car park.
• Map: *OS Explorer OL30 Yorkshire Dales North/Central.*

     Buckden is the first sizeable settlement on the Wharfe, and stands at the meeting place of two high roads from Wensleydale. In medieval times it was the centre of a vast hunting forest, and the *Buck Inn* recalls its former importance in its name. The village stands high above the river on the slope of Buckden Pike, and swift-flowing Buckden Beck carves a deep defile down from the summit. Beside the pub there is a shop, tearooms, gallery and WC.

     Leave the car park not by its exit, instead use a gate at its northern end from where a stony track gently rises up Buckden Rake. This is one of the few confirmed sections of the Roman road that connected the forts at Ilkley and Bainbridge. To this day it remains an excellent route, and provides a perfect picture of the dalehead scene, looking beyond Hubberholme's church tower into Langstrothdale. At the end of the surround of trees it turns right to commence a pleasant, level section, ignoring the Buckden Pike path which soon strikes off to the right.

     Drawing level with the buildings of Cray down to the left, take a bridle-gate in the adjacent wall and down a steep field alongside a wall. Through a gate at the bottom is Cray Gill, crossed by stepping-stones to join the road right next to the pub. Over 1000ft above sea level, this farming hamlet is the last outpost of Wharfedale on the road to Bishopdale and ultimately Wensleydale. This crossing of the fells is known as the Kidstones Pass, the easiest motorable escape out of the upper valley. Cray's one amenity is the welcoming *White Lion*.

Leave by a farm track behind the pub, and follow it up to the left: keep right at an early fork to pass through a limestone floored farmyard above various farm buildings. Just before the last buildings, branch down to the left, and alongside these buildings the path runs through a narrow snicket to emerge in front of the last house. Head along the field top, briefly, then follow the path slanting down this vast tilted pasture. Cray Gill is soon neared below, and becomes a closer companion as the descent continues on lush limestone turf. The beck is an absolute delight, with numerous small waterfalls on show. Towards the bottom a more notable fall is easily missed in the trees, just before crossing a grassy, stone arched footbridge on inflowing Crook Gill.

A more enclosed section leads to a stile into a field, to continue down the beckside through small fields to a stile onto a back road at Stubbing Bridge. Turn right along this narrow road, soon with the company of the River Wharfe to lead along to Hubberholme. Barely even a hamlet, it claims two famous buildings. St. Michael's church is a gem, with the sparkling Wharfe running almost past its very door - see also Walk 2. In an idyllic setting across the river is the whitewashed and timeless *George Inn,* whose snug interior boasts stone flagged floors.

Across the bridge, double back left along the road. After about half a mile take a gate on the left to follow a track to the riverbank. This soon narrows into a nicer path leading downstream to Buckden Bridge. Join the road to re-cross the river back into the village.

4³⁄4 miles   from Buckden

An exhilarating ascent to a mountain top.

• Start: Village centre (GR: 942772).
National Park car park.
• Map: OS Explorer OL30 Yorkshire Dales North/Central..

Turning your back on the *Buck Inn*, tearooms, shop and WC, leave the car park by a gate at the northern end, a broad track rising away. Leave it at once, however, at a sign pointing *'to Starbotton and Buckden Lead Mine'*. This National Trust path doubles faintly back up the grassy bank to a gate. The path continues away, dropping down to Buckden Beck. Turn down as if to re-enter the village, but cross the beck above a 'private' bridge and climb the track rising away. This doubles back uphill away from the beck, rejoining the wall which it shadows away on a raking course. The super old mine track slants unfailingly up the colourful flank with outstanding views over the dale. After a steep section it become greener and runs to a gateway. Gentler graded, the track rises across the pastures until faced by a boundary wall. Here it doubles back left to rise to a guidepost where it meets the Starbotton miners' path.

Continue up this more inviting way, which after a little zigzag resumes its slant. Ultimately it reaches a gate in a descending wall, then levels out: within 50 yards is a fork. While the more obvious one slants up to the right, yours is the fainter one straight ahead, through a crumbled wall and along to a sturdy wall corner. Straight ahead is the Pike. Advance a few paces with the wall and take a stile in it to resume on a good little path on the other side. When the wall drops away into the gill, the path contours straight ahead, passing through an old wall to reveal the lead mine just ahead. The remains of Buckden Lead Mine occupy the very head of Buckden Beck, and are reached on the course of a little tramway leading out from an arched level. Buckden village is in view down at the very foot of the gill.

Resume by rising briefly left to an ascending wall, then a clear path quickly slants off to the right, rising above the workings to a wall corner. By now Fountains Fell, Penyghent and Ingleborough have appeared to the west. The path swings right to rise more gently, meeting a wall to ease out at a corner stile in the wall along Buckden Pike's summit ridge. This earns a big new view ahead, dominated by Great Whernside, also featuring Little Whernside and Penhill. Turn left for a two minute stroll to a stile back over the wall to the cairn and OS column at 2303ft/702m on the summit of Buckden Pike. Its virtues as a viewpoint are in its distant prospects, which are truly extensive. Most of the major Dales summits are visible in the western sector, while to the east, moors give way to the flat plains.

Descent begins by heading north with the wall on a rebuilt path, which soon includes a short stone-built length. The path soon leaves the wall to start a long slant down the fellside, moist in part but allowing you to fully savour the Langstrothdale scene. The going improves as the path enters a string of moorland pastures at a bridle-gate. The hamlet of Cray is seen in its idyllic location directly below. This diagonal course is maintained through several old walls, including passing beneath a limestone scar. At the bottom it merges into the path running along Buckden Rake. Turn left through a gate and follow this old way all the way back. Initially a level green way, it swings stonily down to the left for the final stage back into the car park.

5 miles   from Buckden

**Historic mineworkers' paths on the flanks of
Buckden Pike, with a leisurely riverside finish.**

• Start: Village centre (GR: 942772).
National Park car park.
• Map: OS Explorer OL30 Yorkshire Dales North/Central.

Turning your back on the *Buck Inn*, tearooms,
shop and WC, depart the car park by a gate at the northern end, where a broad track rises away. Leave it at once,
however, as directed by a sign pointing 'to Starbotton and
Buckden Lead Mine'. This National Trust path doubles
faintly back up the grassy bank to a gate in a fence. The
path continues away, dropping to Buckden Beck flowing
over rocky slabs. Turn down as if to re-enter the village,
but cross the beck just above a 'private' bridge and climb
the track rising away. This quickly doubles back uphill away
from the beck, rejoining the wall which it largely shadows
away on a raking course. This old mine track known as
Eastside Road rises consistently across the colourful
slope, initially with a fine bird's-eye view over the village.
This super ascent slants all the way up the steep
flank with outstanding views over the dale. After a steeper section it become greener and runs to a gateway. Now
gentler graded, the track rises steadily across the pastures until faced by a solid boundary wall. Here it doubles
back sharply left to rise by the previous wall to a guidepost where it meets the miners' path from Starbotton to
the lead mines. At around 1510ft/460m, this is the walk's

high point, with a fine view updale to Langstrothdale, including Hubberholme church.

Though the old track is the clearer way, it is time to double back right for Starbotton. The path is very faint as it slants gently across to a stile in that boundary wall, then on through a reedy tract before improving (intermittent marker posts assist), always slanting gently right and on through gaps in old walls. At the end it drops to a small gate in a sturdy descending wall. Part way down, the now super green path reveals the huddle of Starbotton on the dale floor. It continues down to a gate in the bottom corner onto the firm track of Walden Road. Turn down this for a steep drop into Starbotton, soon becoming enclosed. At the bottom it doubles back to bridge Cam Gill Beck. Across, either turn right for the *Fox & Hounds* pub and main road, or left on back lanes to emerge at the southern end of the village.

At the far end of the village a gate on the right sends a broad, walled pathway running directly to the river. A long wooden footbridge carries you high above the Wharfe, then turn upstream on a super path through idyllic surrounds. When the river swings off to the right, continue straight ahead along a wallside old way. At a crumbling barn, continue to a footbridge on a stream for a brief enclosed spell. Emerging, the firm path continues, bearing left and across a field centre. Keep straight on, a track forming which soon slants up to meet a firmer track. Advance along this to a barn, and a little further the path is sent down to a gate near a wall-corner from where it drops down to the returning riverbank. The Wharfe is now followed tightly all the way to Buckden Bridge, largely on a low embankment. Buckden village is immediately in front now. A stile alongside the bridge admits onto the road. Cross the bridge to finish.

4½ miles   from Starbotton

Old upland ways on the flanks of Buckden Pike.

• *Start: Village centre (GR: 953746).*
Limited roadside parking at Kettlewell end.
• *Map: OS Explorer OL30 Yorkshire Dales North/Central.*

Starbotton sits midway between Kettlewell and Buckden, and is usually only visited for refreshment at the attractive *Fox & Hounds* pub. Off the main road however are charming corners featuring 17th century cottages. Starbotton sits astride swift-flowing Cam Gill Beck, which cuts a deep groove in the flank of Buckden Pike: in 1686 it was swollen by a deluge causing disastrous flooding in the village. This walk is a circuit of the beck's little side valley.

Leave the main road by a narrow lane alongside the pub. At the first chance fork left on a rough road over a bridge to start an immediately steep ascent. The track doubles back above a restored bank, rising between walls to emerge into the open. Simply remain on this track as it rises up, with the side valley of Cam Gill Beck spread ahead. Ignore a path off left to Buckden Lead Mine, and continue up. Your track is known as Walden Road, an old inter-valley trade route. Passing through a gateway, the side valley is better revealed as the climb becomes gentler. Across to the right is the ruined chimney of Starbotton Smelt Mill.

The track works back to the left-hand wall to rise with it for some time. When it turns off the track continues up to an old wall junction. Through the gateway it now has a crumbling right-hand wall for company. When the track forks left up the fell, remain on the wallside path. Moist sections precede a gateway in an old cross-wall, above which the path commences a traverse across the fell as a superb hollowed way. It passes above mining spoil to a gate in a sturdy wall that ranges around this dalehead. Just above it you pass a covered, circular shaft of appreciable depth. A few steps further is a large cairn, just above which is the turning point beneath Starbotton Fell. Leave the track for a softer path forking right across fell-like terrain, the walk's high point. As Starbotton Fell Road this runs through a gateway and on to a gate in a sturdy wall. Beyond this a moist section is encountered before another wall, to reach a mining site under Starbotton Out Moor.

Keeping right of it the track improves to contour above a minor bank. A brief glimpse of Great Whernside's summit ridge is seen ahead. Remain on this until the next gateway, past which the bridlepath forks distinctly down to the right (the green way continues to a fence-stile, on above a quarried edge and down to the wall below). Resume the contour on a thin path by the wall below, through a gate in a fence and on until the higher track slants down through the wall. Turn down with it to join the firm track of Starbotton Cam Road just as it becomes enclosed.

The 'road' names given to various green tracks on the fells is a sign of their importance in times past, when they served functional tasks, often simply to reach peat grounds and lead workings. Their well-laid courses were designed for easy descent with the spoils. Turn right down this track all the way to the village. Buckden Pike is now better appreciated across Cam Gill Beck, while Birks Fell forms a dark wall across the main valley. Eventually the old way absorbs an access track to drop down to the back of the village. Go straight across on a side lane to rejoin the main road, or go right for the pub.

4³⁄4 miles   from Kettlewell

A short climb to earn classic Upper Wharfedale views, and a delightful valley return.

• *Start: Village centre (GR: 968722).*
National Park car park.
• *Map: OS Explorer OL30 Yorkshire Dales North/Central.*

      Kettlewell is the hub of Upper Wharfedale, a junction of roads and natural halting place. It straddles its own beck which drains the slopes of Great Whernside, lined by some delectable cottages and gardens as it races through the village. As well as the *Racehorses, Blue Bell* and *Kings Head* pubs, there are shops, tearooms, WC and a youth hostel.

      Leave by crossing the bridge on the Wharfe at the village entrance, and turning sharp right to where two different paths head away. Take the upper track slanting to a gate, from where it heads away alongside a wall. Ignore the branch path slanting up to the Slit, bound for Arncliffe, and remain on the main track. It bears left in front of a clump of trees, crosses a tiny beck and then commences a zigzag climb, ignoring lesser branches. At once there is a superb Upper Wharfedale panorama, to Starbotton backed by Buckden Pike, and back over Kettlewell to Great Whernside. Before long the track eases out and runs on through several old walls to reveal the buildings at Moor End just ahead. Up to the left are spoil heaps from old lead workings, matched by similar ones on a shelf directly across the valley.

Sheep farm turned outdoor centre, isolated Moor End is the highest point of the walk. Rise above the house on a grassy track to a gate in the top corner. Ignore the track continuing up, and go right a few yards to another gate. Through this cross the sloping field centre on a faint path, through a gate at the end and on through a smaller field to a gate through which is a fork. Take the main path slanting down to pass through a bridle-gate in the wall below. This junction with the Arncliffe-Starbotton bridle-way marks a super moment, reveling again in views over the meandering Wharfe to a good combination of Starbotton village, Cam Gill Beck and Buckden Pike. The splendid path runs above the steep drop to the valley before starting a slant to the dale floor, much of it in fine old woodland. Emerging, the path maintains the slant alongside a wall, entering a lichen-covered walled section where it swings right by an old barn to a wooden footbridge on the Wharfe.

If detouring to Starbotton, cross the bridge and follow the walled path to the village. Commence the return leg by turning downstream, the way, for the most part, being pretty obvious. Though the path can be occasionally faint, it is never more than a field's length from the river. When the Wharfe engages in several acute bends, the path tends to short-cut these. Early on, Moor End is seen seemingly delicately perched on the skyline directly ahead.

Through a string of intervening walls at Haw Fields the way becomes a track, intermittently enclosed by walls. Crossing a tiny stream at the end of this section beyond a working barn, take a kissing-gate to the left and a part enclosed path resumes. This merges with the river-bank opposite the village school. When a concrete section ends take a gate on the right and on the fieldside, soon returning for a final riverside section. The path rises to a track at the end to rejoin the road alongside the bridge.

8 —————— PROVIDENCE POT

3³⁄4 miles   from Kettlewell

A beckside ramble with a contrastingly open return.

• Start: Village centre (GR: 968722).
National Park car park.
• Map: OS Explorer OL30 Yorkshire Dales North/Central.

From the car park head into the village and leave
the main road before the bridge by the two hotels, turning
on the road to the right. Fork left at the maypole towards
the church, and at the *Kings Head* turn right on a lane
alongside the beck. At a shapely bridge the lane becomes a
track, and just a little further it crosses Dowber Gill Beck.
Here leave it by turning up a little beckside path to a stile
in the adjacent wall. Now turn right to begin a long mile and
a quarter in very close company with the beck.

After an early ladder-stile a grand path runs into
the valley's tight confines. The beck occasionally slides
over rocky shelves, while Great Whernside's upper slopes
appear on the skyline ahead. Closer to hand on the opposite
slope, a lead mining site includes spoil heaps, ruins and a
distinctive grassy rake. Further, a cliff directly above the
path unleashes a sizeable spring, gushing out to supply the
greater part of the beck: indeed, above here its course is
often bone-dry. The unmistakable site of Providence Pot is
gained either by crossing the beck just before it, or
remaining on the enterprising left bank path. This is one of
the Dales' better-known potholes, well sited in the centre
of the beck. A manhole cover guards the vertical entrance.
The slopes above are scarred with old lead workings.

Directly behind is the meeting of twin becks beneath rougher slopes, but your path is the clear one up the left-hand slope alongside the pothole. Re-cross the beck and ascend this super path through bracken, giving superb views down the side valley and back across to mine workings opposite. Though not currently recorded as a definitive right of way, this path has been in use since time immemorial. Higher up, the path takes advantage of a distinctive dry ditch to ascend by. This levels out to reveal the bouldery Hag Dyke Edge up ahead, with Great Whernside's high skyline summit ridge back to the right; then quickly, just ahead, Hag Dyke. A thin path advances to the house, taking a gate in front and a small gate to the left of the building to emerge at the front. At some 1500ft, Hag Dyke is one of the highest buildings in the country, and since 1947 has been put to use as a scouts' outdoor centre.

Follow the access track out through a gate, then immediately leave it for a broad, grassy path dropping half-left. At once its course down these splendid moor-grass pastures can be discerned almost all the way, keeping for the most part just above the well-defined drop to your outward route. There is an early glimpse of Kettlewell in the bottom. The path drops through a collapsed wall and down to a small gate, along a wallside to a stile and on to another small gate. As the wall climbs away and open slopes take over, the path is now firmly atop the steep drop to Dowber Gill. A marker post on the end sees the descent proper begin. The path slants right, away from the gill, down to a gateway, then winds down to a gateway in a crumbling wall, and a distinct grassy fork. Bear right to a stile and down this last pasture on a super green way to rejoin the outward route at Dowber Gill Beck. The finish can be varied by crossing the bridge by the old chapel to follow another, parallel back road into the village centre.

2³⁄₄ miles   from Kettlewell

Don't feel insulted by the mileage, it's a mini-classic.

• *Start: Village centre (GR: 968722).*
   National Park car park.
• *Map: OS OS Explorer OL2, Yorkshire Dales South/West.*
  or *OS Explorer OL30 Yorkshire Dales North/Central.*

Kettlewell is the hub of Upper Wharfedale, a junction of roads and natural halting place. It straddles its own beck which drains the slopes of Great Whernside, lined by some delectable cottages and gardens as it races through the village. As well as the *Racehorses, Blue Bell* and *Kings Head* pubs, there are shops, tearooms, WC and a youth hostel. Footpaths radiate from Kettlewell to all points of the compass, and one could spend a richly-varied holiday week here without the need of any transport.

Leave the village by crossing the bridge over the Wharfe at the entrance, and within a few steps take a slim stile on the left. Drop to the river and head downstream to the first of an assortment of stiles. These come in various guises, but simply keep to the faint path on a parallel course with the river. Several springs are crossed and the walking is delightful as the Wharfe is followed, sometimes with an old wall between, but largely more intimately. The river is enchanting company, with dippers in evidence, while Knipe Wood adds further colour up to the right. This happy arrangement continues until the path swings uphill towards the road as an old walled way. Just a few paces before this are the stepping-stones that are the walk's turning point.

A series of sturdy concrete blocks should ensure a straightforward river crossing. If the water is dangerously high, then turn round and retrace your steps - no real penance! Across, turn back upstream on the grassy path of Lovers Lane, less romantically titled Hawkswick Head Lane on the map. This super path firmly shadows the river, enclosed by field boundaries all the way. All too soon this spell ends, as the path enters a narrow walled way to rise onto the back road linking Kettlewell and Conistone. Note that a stile on the left sends an alternative path back to the riverbank, and then all the way back to the bridge.

On the minor road, meanwhile, turn right for a few minutes, just as far as a kink where the Dales Way is signed through a gate on the left. Just two minutes further to the right, incidentally, is Scargill House, a Christian retreat and conference centre whose Scandinavian style chapel is a familiar Wharfedale landmark.

From the road follow a wall away to a gate, then turn through it to a gate in a kink in the next wall. Here you commence a fascinating course through about a dozen fields within half a mile. Just up above is a wooded limestone scar, while straight ahead is the broad, walled lane of Top Mere Road ascending the tongue behind unseen Kettlewell. Though not generally visible on the ground, your way follows a near straight wall, more than once switching to either side of it.

Kettlewell appears ahead well before finally emerging at the head of a green snicket on the edge of the village, in front of modern housing. Turn down this splendid way to a T-junction, with the churchyard straight in front. Either pass through here for a look round, or turn right along the enclosed track onto a back lane. Go left to the *Kings Head* and on through the village to finish, passing the village stocks and war memorial just after the maypole.

4³⁄₄ miles   from Halton Gill

Easy walking in a remote corner of the Dales.

• *Start: Village centre (GR: 880764). Car park by green.*
• *Map: OS Explorer OL30 Yorkshire Dales North/Central.*

     Halton Gill is the first sizeable settlement in Littondale. Its cluster of sombre grey buildings includes a centuries-old chapel and even a grammar school, both now private dwellings. From the junction by the green turn down the Stainforth road and over Halton Gill Bridge, then leave by a stile on the right to descend steps to the riverbank. Accompany the Skirfare upstream through the occasional gate or stile. After a pair of plank bridges, take a stile in the adjacent fence to resume upstream to a wall-stile. This is delightful rambling as the riverbank opens out, with a particularly lovely moment where the river tumbles over limestone ledges. A little further, the path squeezes between sheep pens and river to emerge onto the road at Foxup Bridge. Here the moorland streams of Foxup Beck and Cosh Beck combine to create the Skirfare.

     Turn left along the road, briefly, and leave by a gate opposite Foxup Bridge Farm, with its shapely arched bridge. A track winds up the field to a gate at the top. Looking back over the farm's setting note in particular the landscape immediately updale, where green fields, drystone walls and barns on the southern side of Cosh Beck contrast with sombre brown moorland on the north side. The now faint track ascends a large pasture towards a gate in the rising wall.

At this bridleway junction don't pass through, but continue up the grassy track. It levels out to contour left to a gate in the corner above limestone outcrops. Through this head away just above the left-hand wall, which drops away but leaves the splendid grassy path to march on. Grand views look down the dale and across to Halton Gill nestling beneath Horse Head Moor. Ahead is the dark wall of Darnbrook Fell, beyond the unseen Penyghent Gill. Remaining level, a large pasture is crossed to another gate, the path then running on above the low outcrops of Hesleden Bergh to merge with the Stainforth road.

Turn right on the open road, with the side valley of Penyghent Gill ahead beneath Fountains Fell. Pass through a cattle-grid and continue along the road, with Penyghent majestic ahead. The road rises slightly to where a fence comes up from the left. At this point take a stile in the fence and double back down with it. Enjoying this level fence-side path above fine gill scenery, don't forget to look back to Penyghent presiding over the upper gill. Further on, fence and path drop to Nether Hesleden. From a stile a fine green track winds down to a gate between the houses. Go left along the front of one house, with its 1748 datestone.

Follow the drive out the few steps to a gate, just past which take a stile on the left. Continue briefly parallel with the drive, then slant up left to a stile. Advance across the field centre to a gate, and on in the same fashion until Halton Gill is revealed ahead. A stile leads to a ruinous barn, from where the path, never more than faint, commences to run through innumerable stile/gate combinations, regularly shadowed by the chain of Heber Side Barns. Ultimately, when having crossed a stile to find a wall heading away, this ushers the way right, on a slant down to the riverbank. This ensures a fine finish for the few minutes upstream to steps back onto Halton Gill's bridge.

4^{1}2 miles   from Arncliffe

Delectable valley paths on this flattest of walks!

• *Start: Village centre (GR: 931718). Roadside parking.*
• *Map: OS Explorer OL30, Yorkshire Dales North/Central.*

Arncliffe is one of the most attractive villages in the Dales, its characterful houses stood back in relaxed manner from a spacious green. The unpretentious *Falcon* maintains this mood, the only pub in the area to serve its ale directly from the barrel. St. Oswald's church, with its 500-year old tower, occupies a beautiful riverside setting.

From the green head west on the Malham road. After the bridge on Cowside Beck, take a walled track in front. This ends at a stile where stone flags negotiate a moist corner. Cross to a stile near the left corner, then cross a vast field where a wooden slab bridges a modest trickle at the end. Through a gate behind, the path bears right to approach the Skirfare. Advancing upstream, the river wanders off as the path keeps on to a choice of stiles. Continue through a gateway in an old wall, and on to a stile at which you enter Scoska Wood nature reserve: the slopes above support the largest surviving natural ash, rowan wood in the Dales. The river curves back in to join the grassy path, which leaves the reserve through a gate to which you will return. For now, cross the river by a series of massive stone blocks, only in spate are these impassable.

Across, resume upstream on a good path along the wooded bank to reach an impasse. Take the stile alongside and leave the river on an inviting snicket. This swings left and before long take a stile on the right and follow the right-hand wall to a stile in it. Continue on the other side to a stile back onto the lane as it becomes a narrow footway. Go straight on the tight footway to quickly abandon it again, at a pair of stiles to enter a field on the left. A gate at the far end accesses yet another walled track, rapidly reverting to footpath width. Further, a track crosses over, though merely to pass between fields. Just ahead, again continue along a stony, tight walled way. When it becomes overgrown, a stile makes escape into a field on the left. Slant right, through a stile and across a larger field to a small gate onto the road entering Litton.

Though second largest village in the dale, it gave its name to this valley once known as Amerdale. First building encountered is the homely *Queens Arms*. Go left through the village past the tiny Post office and leave the road just beyond the phone box, down a drive to the left. Bear left of a wall at lovely Elbeck House (1707 lintel) to a footbridge on the Skirfare. The river is often dry here, having gone subterranean further upstream. Turn left to a stile, then cross to a small gate. Turn right alongside a stream, crossing it at a wooden bridge onto a drive.

Go left a few paces then take a gate on the right. Cross the field to another gate then go left with the wall, continuing to a corner bridle-gate to rejoin the tree-lined river. A delightful path squeezes downstream alongside a lichen-covered wall, finally emerging at a gate to resume through fields. Though at times faint underfoot, the way is obvious as it heads on through the fields. Through an old wall the river bends away a little: cross a stone slab on a tiny stream and on to a bend of the river. The outward route is rejoined by passing through a small gate in the fence alongside the stepping-stones. Return the way you came, a lovely walk back to Arncliffe.

3 miles   from Conistone

A superb limestone ravine leads to a classic viewpoint.

· *Start: Conistone Bridge (GR: 979674). Roadside parking.*
· *Map: OS Explorer OL2, Yorkshire Dales South/West.*

Conistone is an attractive little village avoided by the main road which heads updale just half a mile distant, across the river at Kilnsey: even from this distance the famous crag loses none of its grandeur. Every piece of stone in Conistone's cottages matches the natural land- scape of the village's hinterland, and a number of cottages bear dated stone lintels going back to the 17th century. A tall, slender maypole graces the village centre, sprouting from a tiny island of seats. Conistone is also home to a pony trekking centre.

From the bridge enter the village, and at the road junction set off left along the Kettlewell road. Then turn immediately right on an access track across a wide green. From the gate at the far end by the old school, the village is left behind and through successive gates the path enters the foot of Gurling Trough. The way becomes stony under- foot as it heads into what proves to be a classic example of a dry limestone valley: this is the start of Conistone Dib, initially up through a dry waterfall and then tightly con- fined by imposing buttresses. The path is squeezed out like a champagne cork to pass through a long, green pasture. When the slopes close in again, ignore a branch path escap- ing to the right, and stay with the wall for a short, stony climb to the head of the valley.

At the very top a ladder-stile precedes a simple hands-on scramble to leave you emphatically on the top. Just above, take a stile on the right, and then turn left on a grassy track to a gate which gives access to the wide track of the Bycliffe Road. A superb limestone pavement sits just above: at its far side is an old limekiln.

While this track is to be your return route, first cross straight over at the path crossroads, on the broad grassy way pointing to Kettlewell. This inviting path runs beneath a modest limestone scar, quickly revealing the fortress-like Conistone Pie directly ahead. On reaching a ladder-stile, vacate the main path and ascend the little path to the now adjacent 'Pie'.

Conistone Pie is a minor upthrust of rock crowned by a cairn, and makes a conspicuous Wharfedale landmark. It commands a superb view of the fork of the arrow-like valleys of the Wharfe and its identical sidekick the Skirfare, emerging from Littondale. Across the valley is the often dark shadow of Kilnsey Crag, with the ancient highway of Mastiles Lane climbing high past it. On the dale floor meanwhile is the secretive Amerdale Dub, confluence of the Skirfare with the Wharfe (Amerdale is the old name for Littondale).

Return to the track of the Bycliffe Road and turn right along it - now as Scot Gate Lane - soon descending Wassa Bank past the T.V. mast which has been in sight at various stages of the walk. Becoming largely surfaced, the access road winds down to join the Conistone-Kettlewell road, with the village only minutes along to the left. En route you pass the hidden church of St. Mary, which retains some Norman features. A churchyard tablet remembers six students tragically killed in a flood in Mossdale Cavern, high on the fells above Conistone Dib, in 1967.

4³⁄₄ miles   from Grassington

**A splendid woodland nature reserve is followed
by a delectable riverbank stroll.**

•*Start: Village centre (GR: 002639).
National Park car park on Hebden Road.*
•*Map: OS Explorer OL2, Yorkshire Dales South/West.*

From the cobbled square head up the street past
the *Devonshire Arms* to a crossroads by the Institute, and
go left on Chapel Street to leave the bustling scene of
shops, pubs and cafes behind. Part way on turn right up
Bank Lane, which quickly swings left as a walled track. At a
path junction towards the end, turn left through a small
gate, over a plank bridge and across the field to a stile.
From the stile go left to another stile just below. While
the Dales Way follows the track right, cross straight over
to a narrow stile in the wall opposite. Bear right across a
large, undulating field to find a similar stile onto Cove Lane.
Ahead is a pleasing arrangement of field walls and barns in
front of Grass Wood. Accompany the green lane to its
demise, and take the right-hand gate. Cross to the far end
of the field, and on to a stile into Grass Wood.

This largest remnant of native broadleaved woodland in the Dales is run by Yorkshire Wildlife Trust. Just
after entering the wood is the site of a Celtic settlement
identified by low, lichen covered stones. A good path heads
up through the trees, keeping right on a broader path at
the first fork. The path rises steadily for some time to
reach a brow near a wall corner. Now level, the broad,

firmer path runs through a clearing, alongside a distinctive trough to a crosspaths. The thin path left offers a short diversion up a low limestone scar to the Iron Age hillfort of Fort Gregory, its distinctive foundations dating from AD70.

Back at the crossroads resume along the main path, briefly, towards a broader clearing, but leave the wide track for a less firm one branching right. It maintains a level course through trees with a moss covered limestone pavement on the left, before descending towards the far end of the wood. After a sharp left turn the descent gathers pace, merging into the wide track forsaken earlier. Examples of woodland management feature coppicing, the harvesting of hazel and ash. Continuing down, with the boundary wall now close to hand there are views north to Kilnsey Crag. The track ends at Grass Wood Lane.

Head left a short distance, and a stile into the Woodland Trust's Lower Grass Wood precedes the public path. A super path passes through a stile and along the wood edge to the Wharfe's bank. Looming eerily high on the opposite bank is Netherside Hall, a school. Resume downstream, a super path soon rises onto a higher bank, and merges with another. Further, at a cross-paths, bear right past a limestone boulder on the main one back down to the river and along to a stile out of the wood. Delightful riverbank walking on open pastures leads to a wooded knoll. Here is Ghaistrill's Strid, a rare moment of turbulence for the Wharfe. A seat invites a longer pause as the river is channelled through a ravine amongst rocky shelves.

The path runs to a stile just ahead, into a short enclosed spell above the lively river. The Wharfe's bank is regained to resume across a footbridge on a stream and on to approach Grassington Bridge. A track at the top corner runs to a gate in front of a grassy area with seats next to the road. Turn up the roadside footway to finish.

4³⁄4 miles   from Grassington

Lush limestone pastures, extensive views, rich history.

•*Start: Village centre (GR: 002639).*
National Park car park on Hebden Road.
•*Map: OS Explorer OL2, Yorkshire Dales South/West.*

Grassington is capital of Upper Wharfedale, a thriving community with a wide range of pubs, cafes and shops. The cobbled square, with the Upper Wharfedale Folk Museum, is the focal point, but hidden away is enough interest for a day's leisurely exploration. Buildings of character include the Old Hall and the former Town Hall-cum-institute.

From the square head up the street past the *Devonshire Arms* to a crossroads by the institute, and turn left along Chapel Street. Part way on turn right up Bank Lane, which quickly swings left as a walled track. Remain on this to its demise at a stile. Turn left on an inviting green way rising along the slender field. When it opens out at a wall corner, remain with the right-hand wall to slant to the far end. You are now on Kimpergill Hill, surrounded by barely discernable ancient settlements and field systems.

From the stile at the very end, resume with the wall above, slanting across to a stile in the wall above. The good path maintains this steady slant through a couple of old walls in succession, a stile just behind, and on further across a larger pasture. Only half way on it slants up to a stile in the wall above, and rises diagonally again across another sizeable pasture. Here you pass a circular walled dewpond (now dry) created as a water source for cattle in these dry uplands. From a stile at the end the path quickly reveals Bare House just ahead. Great Whernside is also fully revealed beyond, joining fellow height Buckden Pike.

The abandoned farm of Bare House is an isolated landmark. Take the gate to its left and swing right outside the small enclosure behind, around to run on to roofless High Barn. From a gate alongside, a track crosses the field to a gate out onto Downs Pasture. Bear right on this track rising to a gate ahead. This admits to a walled green lane, a splendid stride across the walk's high point. Remain on this all the way to Old Moor Lane on the edge of Yarnbury. En route, the smelt mill chimney on Grassington Moor stands tall ahead. Turn right onto Moor Lane at Yarnbury. Just before the surfaced lane head, the way bridges a sloping tunnel through which ore was hauled from a deep mine level. Just over the wall is the start of a fascinating trail around the lead mining remains, more of which are seen on Walk 15.

Yarnbury House was the 19th century mine agent's office, a busier scene than today! Though you could remain on the road, a short loop takes a stile on the left after it becomes surfaced. Cross to a stile in the opposite wall, left of a gate, then bear gently right up to a stile above. Passing through, you are stood alongside the banks of an ancient circular henge. Resume to the far corner of the field, where a stile re-admits onto Moor Lane. Turn left, and just before a steeper descent starts, take a stile on the right. A trod crosses to a gate in the wall ahead, revealing a fine panorama of the Grassington district. A path descends the steep pasture to a stile in the right-hand wall. Continue down to a corner gate, then resume on the wallside past Intake Lathe to a gate. Grassy Intake Lane is joined, leading down onto an access road at some houses. Cross straight over, through a stile and down a snicket to emerge onto the foot of Bank Lane. Retrace steps back into the centre.

-⟨15⟩——— GRASSINGTON MOOR

4³⁄₄ miles   from Yarnbury

Absorbing lead mining remains in a fine upland setting.

•*Start: Yarnbury stands at the top of Moor Lane, 1¹⁄₂ miles out of Grassington (GR:015658). Roadside parking.*
•*Map: OS Explorer OL2, Yorkshire Dales South/West.*

Grassington Moor was a major centre of Dales' lead mining. The industry peaked in the early 19th century, and ended completely before that century did. At 1150ft above sea-level, this bleak setting of Yarnbury would have been much busier when Yarnbury House was the mine agent's office - an old weigh house stands in the grounds.

From the road end turn back along the road just as far as a stile on the left behind a seat. Cross to find a stile in the wall beyond, just left of a gate. Rise away to a wall corner, then continue with the wall on the right down a lengthy rough pasture, an improving path passing small quarry workings. From the gate at the bottom continue gently down, a grassy track bearing slightly away from the wall, passing the distinct bowl of a former dam. From a gate in the very bottom corner rise gently away to the far end, where there is a gate just short of the very corner. Drop onto a clear track just beyond, and double back left on it down to High Garnshaw House.

Remain on the track (Tinkers' Lane) past the farm, soon rising to a gate on the brow ahead. The way becomes intermittently open and then enclosed by walls: the chimney on the moor is straight ahead. Slanting down the fieldside on a reedy old way, look across into the deep cleft of Bolton Gill to see the dark shadow of a former winding shaft from around 1856 near the top. The final stage is enclosed again as the track zigzags down onto the floor of Hebden Gill, scene of much mining activity.

Through the gate turn left, immediately through another gate and along the firm track. This twice fords the tiny beck, pulls through mining debris, drops again, then ascends past a limekiln. Climbing out of the gill to a fork, go right through a gate, and ascending still with extensive spoil heaps across to the left (ignore any branch tracks) up to a junction with the broad track of Duke's New Road.

At Duke's New Road it is just minutes (left) back to Yarnbury, but the moorland loop awaits: turn right to a gate from where the track contours across heathery Grassington Moor. An embankment of an old dam at the upper reach of the gill leads to a gate at Cupola Corner. Cupola Smelt Mill was built in 1793 and fired by locally won coal. A mile-long system of flues took fumes from the mill to the lofty chimney. The definitive path ends just before the mill: a notice explains the access situation, though always be aware of danger from mineshafts and unstable buildings. Through here the track rises away, but at the first bend leave it by bearing right and ascending alongside (not on) the flue to the chimney. The chimney stands at the top of the flue system, and was preserved in 1971.

Return to Cupola Corner and back across the embankment. Just across it turn right on a path to a gate in the wall, accessing Old Moor Lane. Turn left up its wide walled course, over the brow to reveal Yarnbury just below. Yards before the end, the way bridges a sloping tunnel through which ore was hauled from a deep mine level. A Lead Mine Trail offers a detailed exploration of countless features of interest in the vicinity: this makes a separate walk well worth undertaking.

4³4 miles   from Grassington

Exceptionally easy field and riverbank walking.

•Start: National Park Centre (GR: 002637)
on Hebden Road (B6265). Car park.
•Map: OS Explorer OL2, Yorkshire Dales South/West.

From the square head up the street past the *Devonshire Arms*. At the top, in front of the Institute, leave the bustling scene of shops, pubs and cafes behind and turn right on Low Lane, then left up High Lane. This stony walled way rises to leave the houses behind, leveling out as a fine grassy track to eventually emerge into a field. Advance along the track just as far as a wall corner, then as it drops away, take a thin path across the field to a similar wall corner and on to the end, where a track comes back in. Pass through the gate and on the wallside, but just short of the corner slant left to a stile in the wall ahead. Cross to another and across an unkempt enclosure. From the stile at the end, cross two further fields to enter the grounds of the old Grassington Hospital. An exclusive residential development has replaced the hospital where patients came to recover from the likes of tuberculosis.

Head away on the path, crossing the access road and on by flower-rich meadows. Back into trees at the far end, is a path crossroads. Go straight on, through the stile and across a farm road. From a stile at the end bear right to another end stile. A thin path runs through a tapering pasture to a gate in the corner, then runs between walls to the road at the top of Hebden. Turn left for the village.

Passing the *Clarendon* pub, at the crossroads go right into the village, with a Post office/shop and WC. Just past the old school, a kissing-gate on the left sends a path descending to Hebden Beck. Further downstream the path crosses a footbridge at a weir, and on beneath a fish farm to a track junction. Take neither, but a level path heading away between the two branches. This becomes enclosed and runs on to modern houses. Follow the drive out onto a road. Turn right over Hebden Beck, and just before the road starts to climb, a gate on the left sends a path across to the Wharfe's bank above a suspension bridge.

Turn upstream on a broad path tracing the serene Wharfe through a shallow trough, briefly passing through a wooded section. Emerging into open pasture, the path avoids a bend of the river by going straight ahead to a footbridge on a stream. Ahead is Linton's church, and the path continues across the field to cross an access track just short of the riverbank. From the gate on the right head away on a rough road. Passing a fish farm it becomes surfaced. Rising away, take a stile on the left at a bend. Slant down the field to the top of a steep bank above the river, opposite the church. Turn upstream, but as the river bends away, keep straight on along the minor bank to a stile. The way runs through two further fields, closing in on the river to reach Linton Falls footbridge.

The bridge makes a perfect vantage point as the Wharfe erupts into a rare moment of anger to tumble over limestone ledges. On the other bank, contrast the old mill-workers' terraces with the modern housing occupying the site of a mill demolished in the 1980s. After surveying the scene, return to your bank and turn right up the walled footway of Sedber Lane. Note the barn on the right with its 1682 datestone and stylish lintels. Towards the top a gate admits into the main car park.

3¹2 miles   from Hebden

Good paths discover a fascinating lead mining past.

•*Start: Village centre (GR: 026631).
Roadside parking at top end of village, off B6265.*
•*Map: OS Explorer OL2, Yorkshire Dales South/West*

Hebden village has a Post office/shop, WC and the *Clarendon* pub. From the crossroads with the Pateley Bridge road at the top of the village at Town Hill, note a lovely scene of cottages around an old bridge before you head northwards along the unsigned road. This becomes a bridleway after the last cottage, though remains surfaced to its demise at Hole Bottom. En route it enjoys the charming surrounds of Hebden Beck before rising over a small brow to drop to the few buildings at Hole Bottom.

Here fork right, on past the last house and right again, through a gate into the open surrounds of Hebden Gill. A good track crosses a stone arched bridge and turns upstream beneath the colourful, craggy flank of Care Scar. Remain on this old miners' track all the way along the gill, passing through several gates as the old mining site is reached. Ruins and spoil heaps abound as the surrounds open out at the deep enclave of inflowing Bolton Gill.

This is the turning point. Crossing neither beck, turn right up a grassy path immediately before it. Looking up the deep cleft of this side valley, a dark shadow near the top is a restored winding shaft from around 1856. Cross over a stony track and resume up a contrastingly inviting green one. As the dark arch of the winding shaft appears above, a thin but obvious way doubles back to the right. The stone kerbed former watercourse contours round the steep hillside to another arched level. Here the stony track returns, to now run more invitingly to a gate ahead. Looking back, the upper reach of Hebden Gill merges into Grassington Moor, its smelt mill chimney in evidence.

Leaving the mining scene behind, a grassy path heads through two further gates, rising very gently to be ushered by a wall to a gate at the far end. This admits onto grassy moor, and a super path runs to the end. Conspicuous to the left is the grassy dam of Mossy Moor Reservoir, a relic from mining days, though the water is not seen until reaching the top. The gate behind accesses Mossy Moor, and the path runs to a brow. A little further it meets a stony drive to Scar Top House just across to the right.

Though normal practice is to cross the cattle-grid and down the drive to stop at the house gate, the true path is on the drive away for a minute, then doubles acutely back above the wall to a corner stile. From this cross the drive, don't enter the confines but curve round outside the wall to a gateway at the bottom. This is a splendid moment gaining the edge of Care Scar, with a sudden drop back into Hebden Gill. The dramatic view includes Burnsall Fell and the distant Pendle Hill, with Care Scar's tangle of boulders just to the right. A super little path winds down through bracken to a small gate in the wall below.

A thin trod heads off across contrasting green pasture, then slants to the bottom left corner, meeting the wall and tracing it to the far end. Through a stile advance on a field bottom to a stile at the end, then a grassy way slants down above the beck to a stile at the end. Behind it is a footbridge, but remain on this bank on a path downstream to a row of cottages, passing along the front and up over that attractive bridge to finish.

3³4 miles   from Linton Falls

A simple amble through field and village, full of interest.

•*Start: National Park car park/WC (GR: 001631)*
on cul de sac road to Linton Church.
•*Map: OS Explorer OL2, Yorkshire Dales South/West.*

Head along the lane towards the lovely old church of St. Michael & All Angels, but at the first house turn right up a walled way. Almost at once leave this by a tiny gate on the right. A fieldside path rises away, soon running more gently on to meet the B6160. Go right just a short way and fork left for Linton: note the old stone guidepost. This back road soon drops down into lovely Linton, which boasts a rich assortment of buildings stood back from a sloping green. The *Fountaine Inn* recalls a local benefactor who funded the 18th century almshouses across the green. Through the green runs Linton Beck, crossed by road bridge, clapper bridge, packhorse bridge and ford.

Leave by a track (Well Lane) departing the far side of the road bridge, downstream past a pinfold. This narrows into a footway to emerge into a field. Take the left fork to a bridge on the old Grassington branch line. Across, the path bears right to a belt of trees, then left with the wall to run through a gateway and remain with the wall to join the B6265. Cross with care, going left a few steps to head off along a side road, Moor Lane. Remain on this just as far as a house, after which take a stile on the right. Head away with the wall, and continue through the centre of this large pasture to find a stile towards the far end.

Slant down towards a house ahead, using a stile just past a gate to emerge onto Grysedale Lane at Grysedale Gate.

Turn right, but before the next house leave by a stile on the right. Drop to a stile below, and head away between wall and stream. Opening out, cross to a stile ahead, then over a drive where it bridges Rowley Beck to a stile opposite. This hides a slab bridge on Spiredale Beck, from where bear right to a corner stile. Now bear right to a stile further round, and continue by a line of trees to the next stile. Turn left up the wallside, Threshfield appearing. Towards the end is a stile in the wall, from where bear right across a large field to a stile in front of houses. Advance down the wallside of this small enclosure to a stile on the left, emptying onto a farm track into Threshfield.

At the *Old Hall Inn* cross the B6265 to a side road heading away past the enclosed green. Joining the B6160 at the end, go straight ahead to a gate from where a walled, grassy track heads away. Emerging into a field, a thin path continues along the wallside to a stile at the far end. A leafy enclosed path on the left traces the course of a tramway that brought quarried stone down from Skirethorns, above Threshfield, to meet the Grassington branch line. Cross straight over and turn left on a path alongside modern housing (on the station site), emerging at the end onto the B6265, still in Threshfield. Cross to the shop and turn right, dropping to cross the Wharfe on Grassington Bridge. Immediately over, cross with care to a little gate from where a path heads downstream, passing a couple of weirs as it runs along to Linton Falls. The bridge makes a perfect vantage point as the Wharfe tumbles over limestone ledges. On the other bank, contrast the old mill-workers' terraces with modern housing occupying the site of a mill demolished in the 1980s. Across the bridge a short snicket leads onto the road just short of the car park.

3$\frac{1}{2}$ miles   from Linton Falls

Plenty of interest in and around this lovely village.

• *Start: National Park car park/WC (GR: 001631)*
  on cul de sac road to Linton Church.
• *Map: OS Explorer OL2, Yorkshire Dales South/West.*

Head along the lane towards the lovely old church of St. Michael & All Angels, but at the first house turn right up a walled way. Emerging into a field at the top, ascend to a stile in front of a barn, then continue behind it onto a brow. This is a good little viewpoint for the environs of Linton church. Resume along the bank top to a stile at the far side, then slant right across two small fields to the B6160. Go right a few yards to a gate opposite and rise left to a corner gate. The fields hereabouts - and some seen just across the river - sport well-defined strip lynchets, the cultivation terraces of early farmers. Ascend to a small gate at the top. This admits to a narrow snicket winding up to Thorpe Lane.

Turn right on this narrow byway, ignoring an early path right and continuing beneath Cracoe Fell until the lane drops steeply to a set of drives. Take that right, bound for Ings House. On the little brow, look ahead to see Linton backed by Grass Wood and the updale heights of Birks Fell, Buckden Pike and Great Whernside. Before the house take a stile hidden behind a barn, and cross a couple of fields to join a track. This runs alongside a wall, through a small enclosure at the end and then more firmly along to meet another track at the end. Turn left into a farmyard and right into Linton village. Lovely Linton boasts a rich assortment of buildings stood back from a sloping green. The *Fountaine Inn* recalls a local benefactor who funded the 18th century almshouses across the green. Through the green runs Linton Beck, crossed by road bridge, clapper bridge, packhorse bridge and ford.

Leave by a track (Well Lane) departing from the other side of the road bridge, downstream past a pinfold. This narrows into an enclosed footway to emerge into a field. Take the lower of two departing paths, contouring around the field above the beck and below the old railway. This was the branch line from Skipton to Grassington, which operated from 1902 to 1969: it still comes within a couple of miles, but only to serve a limestone quarry. Through a gate at the end, go beneath a rail underpass out into a field. Threshfield village appears ahead.

A thin path heads diagonally away to a slab bridge on Ings Beck, with a stile behind. The thin way continues, rising into a beech wooded corner to a stile onto the B6160. Cross to a gate just a few yards to the right. From it a path crosses to bridge the old railway, and a broader track curves down to Threshfield School. This fine 17th century building was originally a grammar school. Turn left on the road the short way to a stile on the right. A path doubles back downstream, soon joining the Wharfe to reach the delightful 'miniature' Li'l Emily's Bridge on Captain Beck. Across, turn left on a snicket to Linton Falls footbridge.

The bridge makes a perfect vantage point as the Wharfe erupts into a rare moment of anger to tumble over limestone ledges. On the other bank, contrast the old mill-workers' terraces with the modern housing occupying the site of a mill demolished in the 1980s. After surveying the scene, double back along the snicket and onto the road just short of the car park.

3¹2 miles   from Burnsall

**Riverbank, fieldpaths and a hidden hamlet
in the shadow of Burnsall Fell**

•*Start: Village centre (GR: 032611). Car park.*
•*Map: OS Explorer OL2, Yorkshire Dales South/West.*

        Burnsall's setting is one of near-perfection, with
bridge, green, maypole, church, pub and cottages fusing
into an unforgettable scene by the Wharfe. St. Wilfred's
church dates largely from the 15th century, and alongside
is the lovely village school, founded in 1602 by William
Craven as one of the earliest grammar schools. There are
two pubs, the *Red Lion* and the *Fell*, shop, tearoom and WC.
        From the bridge turn upstream on the village side
of the riverbank, past a hotel car park and immediately into
some fine surrounds. Passing beneath the rear of the upper
village the river soon leads away, and beyond an information
panel the path rises to a knoll to look down on the gorge of
Loup Scar, a very lively section of the Wharfe. Dropping
back to the river, this leads delightfully upstream to reach
the suspension bridge beneath Hebden. Though the walk
doesn't cross it, this is a place to linger. Just before
reaching it, a wooded area features an old stone stairway,
the 'Postman's Steps'. The bridge was constructed in 1885
to replace stepping-stones (known as Hebden Hippings)
that have since been restored immediately downstream.
        Leave by a bridle-gate on the left just before the
bridge, and a steep path climbs the little bank. At the top
look back over this scene, then the path rises more gently

away. From a gate at the top it runs faintly on the wallside heading away, through two further gates. By the time the brow is reached there are good views updale beyond Grass Wood. Continue on to a gate onto the B6160. Across is an old stone guidepost, with hands pointing to Burnsall, Linton and Kilnsey. Cross straight over onto the minor Thorpe Lane leading to Thorpe. On the highest point the Burnsall path is signed off as a walled track on the left, but first advance two minutes further for a brief look at Thorpe.

The farming hamlet of Thorpe has an elusiveness that allegedly kept it hidden from marauding Scots. Romantically titled Thorpe in the Hollow, it shelters between limestone reef knolls and below the overpowering Thorpe Fell. Note the triangular little enclosed green.

Returning to the brow, take the signed path off through a gate and away as a walled track. Part way on it becomes more of a green footway as it drops down. Just five paces before it ends take a stile on the right, and drop down to a bridle-gate at the far end. Head away outside a small wood, and on with the wall to a stile at the end. Across the trickle behind, rise up the low bank and head away again, crossing straight over two fields. Head across the centre of the next field, angling to the wall on the left to find, at the far end, a stile onto stony Badger Lane. Cross straight over and resume to a small brow, revealing Burnsall just ahead. The church tower makes a useful guide, while behind it, Simon's Seat dominates the skyline.

Drop to a stile below, slant right to another in the bottom corner, then march in a straight line towards the village, a string of stiles pointing the way infallibly back. Burnsall Fell looks nice and rugged up above, more so as the end is neared. Another stony track is crossed near the end, past which cross the last field to a gate into a tiny snicket back onto the village street. Turn right for the green.

HILLSIDE GUIDES... cover much of Northern England

Other *Pocket Walks* guides (more available shortly)
·ESKDALE, North York Moors
·AMBLESIDE & LANGDALE, Lake District

Our *Walking Country* range features more great walks...

·WHARFEDALE	·MALHAMDALE	·WENSLEYDALE
·SWALEDALE	·NIDDERDALE	·THREE PEAKS
·HOWGILL FELLS	·TEESDALE	·EDEN VALLEY

·NORTH YORK MOORS, SOUTH
·NORTH YORK MOORS, WEST

·ILKLEY MOOR ·BRONTE COUNTRY ·CALDERDALE
·BOWLAND ·PENDLE & RIBBLE ·WEST PENNINE MOORS

·SOUTHERN PENNINES ·NORTHERN PEAK ·EASTERN PEAK
·CENTRAL PEAK ·SOUTHERN PEAK ·WESTERN PEAK

·LAKELAND FELLS, SOUTH   ·LAKELAND FELLS, EAST
·LAKELAND FELLS, NORTH   ·LAKELAND FELLS, WEST

Long Distance Walks, including
·CLEVELAND WAY ·DALES WAY ·LADY ANNE'S WAY
·COAST TO COAST WALK   ·TRANS-PENNINE WAY

Also available
·YORKSHIRE DALES VISITOR GUIDE
·YORKSHIRE DALES, MOORS & FELLS
·THE HIGH PEAKS OF ENGLAND & WALES

Visit www.hillsidepublications.co.uk
or write for a catalogue